21st
Century
Skills Library

REAL WORLD MATH: PERSONAL FINANCE

LIVING ON
A BUDGET

Cecilia Minden

Cherry Lake Publishing
Ann Arbor, Michigan

Published in the United States of America by Cherry Lake Publishing
Ann Arbor, MI
www.cherrylakepublishing.com

Math Education Adviser: Timothy J. Whiteford, PhD, Associate Professor of Education, St. Michael's College, Colchester, Vermont

Finance Adviser: Ryan Spaude, CFP®, Kitchenmaster Financial Services, LLC, North Mankato, Minnesota

Library of Congress Cataloging-in-Publication Data

Minden, Cecilia.
   Living on a budget / by Cecilia Minden.
      p. cm.—(Real world math)
   ISBN-13: 978-1-60279-004-9
   ISBN-10: 1-60279-004-3
   1. Budgets, Personal—Juvenile literature. 2. Finance, Personal—Juvenile literature. I. Title. II. Series.

   HG179.M5254 2008
   332.024—dc22   2007006960

*Cherry Lake Publishing would like to acknowledge the work of
The Partnership for 21st Century Skills.
Please visit www.21stcenturyskills.org for more information.*

TABLE OF CONTENTS

CHAPTER ONE

WHAT IS A BUDGET?

If you don't think before your spend your money, you may soon have an empty wallet!

On Saturday, Elyse was planning to go to the movies with her friend Kadir. But when she got to the theater, she opened her wallet and discovered she had only $2.00. Her parents had given her $10.00 for her allowance just three days before. What did she buy with her money? She couldn't even remember. She probably bought some snacks, and she thinks she bought a magazine, but she doesn't know where she put it. Elyse's money had slipped through her fingers. She needs a budget.

What is a budget? A budget is a plan for how you are going to use your income to pay for your expenses. It is a written record of how much you earn and what you spend it on. If your income is greater than your expenses, you have a balanced budget. Learning to balance a budget is an important skill in life.

Income is all the money you receive. Your allowance is one type of income. Usually, your allowance increases as you get older. In some families, the amount of your allowance is related

21st Century Content

Savings are an important part of your budget. By putting your savings in a bank, your money can earn you more money. Banks will pay you money, called interest, to keep your savings with them. Even small amounts can add up quickly. Let's say you saved $30 a month and put it in a savings account earning 5 percent interest. At the end of five years, you would have more than $2,000 in your account!

to what jobs you do around the house. Wages are income you receive when working for others. With wages, you get a set amount of money for each hour worked. Gifts are another source of income. You might receive money for birthdays or other special occasions. Allowances, wages, and gifts are three ways that students can receive income.

Expenses are the money you spend. Expenses might include food, clothing, entertainment, donations to charity, and savings.

Balancing your budget isn't hard, but it does take some planning. Let's get started!

REAL WORLD MATH CHALLENGE

Megan's parents give her $20.00 a week as an allowance. On the days that Megan doesn't want to bring lunch from home, she has to use her own money to buy lunch at the school cafeteria. Megan uses $12.00 each week for lunches, donates $2.00 a week to the animal shelter, puts $4.00 in savings, and spends $2.50 on snacks. **What are Megan's weekly expenses? Does she have a balanced budget?**

(Turn to page 29 for the answers)

CHAPTER TWO

WHERE DOES YOUR MONEY GO?

Before you set up a budget, you need to think about what things you spend money on. The most important question to ask about each item is, do I need it? Are the things you buy *needs*, or are they *wants*?

Thinking about what you spend your money on is the first step in creating a budget.

*You need clothing, but you can control how much
of your money you spend on clothes.*

Needs are the things you must have to survive. The most basic needs

are food and water, shelter, and clothing. Other needs include school

supplies and transportation. Wants are things you would like to have

but don't absolutely have to have. These might include CDs, expensive clothing, or tickets to movies or sports events. While donations are important to include, they would also be considered a want. Can you buy everything you want? Probably not. But you can have some of your wants if you plan carefully. When creating a budget, make sure your needs are taken care of first. Then figure out how to pay for the wants that are most important to you.

The first step in creating a budget is determining your income and expenses. Keep a money diary for two weeks. To keep a money diary, write down every item you buy and how much it cost. Use a small notebook so you can carry it with you at all times. It is important to write down every single thing you spend money on. No amount is too small. At the end of two weeks, you should have a good idea of how much money you spend and what you buy with it. This will help you make a budget.

REAL WORLD MATH CHALLENGE

Megan wanted to create a budget. She began by keeping a money diary for two weeks:

Megan's Money Diary for March 1 to March 15

DATE	INCOME	DATE	EXPENSE
March 1	$30.00 for birthday	March 3	$15.00 clothing
			$6.00 movie ticket $7.00 snacks
		March 4	$2.00 donation to animal shelter
March 5	$20.00 allowance	March 5	$12.00 school lunch card
		March 7	$1.65 paper and pencils at the school store
March 10	$7.25 raked leaves for neighbor	March 10	$13.25 for CD
March 12	$20.00 allowance	March 12	$12.00 school lunch card
		March 15	$5.43 souvenir shop at the art museum (field trip)

What was Megan's income from March 1 to March 15?

What were Megan's expenses for that time period?

Which expenses were needs? How much did Megan spend on them?

Which expenses were wants? How much did Megan spend on them?

Did she have a balanced budget?

(Turn to page 29 for the answers)

After making a money diary, Megan has a better idea of her income and expenses. How does she turn that information into a budget?

Keeping track of your income and your expenses is an important step in creating a budget.

CHAPTER THREE

DO THE MATH: CREATE A SIMPLE BUDGET

Whenen making a budget, you need to estimate both your income and

your expenses. Some kinds of income and expenses stay the same from

week to week. These are called fixed income and expenses. You can count

Money for school supplies may be one of your budget's variable expenses.

on getting your allowance or wages from a regular job. This is your fixed income. Fixed expenses might include school lunches, regular donations to charity, or regular deposits into a savings account.

You will also have variable income and expenses. *Variable* means that these amounts will change. You might have more income one week because you were given money as a birthday present. You might have more expenses the following week because you had to buy extra supplies for a school project.

As you're preparing to make a budget, you'll also need to think about your short- and long-term goals. Short-term goals are things you want to be able to buy within a few weeks or months. A short-term goal might be a concert ticket, a DVD, or a computer game. Long-term goals are goals that cost more money and will take many months or even years of saving.

A long-term goal might be a vacation, a bike, or money for college. When you make your budget, you'll want to set aside money for both short- and long-term goals.

To create a budget, make a list of your different expenses. Then divide up your money, putting some in each category on your list. If you stick to your budget, you will not allow yourself to spend more than the amount in that category. Make one column for what you planned to spend and one column for what you actually spent. This helps you keep track of exactly where you spent more than you had budgeted.

In her budget, Megan has planned all her expenses for the next two weeks. Can she stick to her budget?

Let's find out!

REAL WORLD MATH CHALLENGE

Megan set up her budget based on her money diary. She included saving for both short- and long-term goals. Megan wasn't sure if she would be doing any chores for neighbors in the next two weeks, so she left that line blank.

Budget for March 15 to March 31 (2 weeks)

CATEGORY	BUDGETED AMOUNT	ACTUAL AMOUNT	DIFFERENCE
FIXED INCOME			
Allowance $20.00 per week x 2	$40.00		
VARIABLE INCOME			
Chores for neighbors			
TOTAL	$40.00		
FIXED EXPENSES			
School lunches	$24.00		
Donation to animal shelter	$2.00		
Short-term goal	$1.00		
Long-term goal	$1.00		
VARIABLE EXPENSES			
School supplies	$0.75		
Snacks	$1.25		
Entertainment	$10.00		
TOTAL			

What are Megan's total expenses?

Megan decides she wants to save more for her long- and short-term goals. She changes her budget for entertainment to $7.00 and her budget for snacks to $0.75. She puts the rest in savings, dividing it equally between long- and short-term goals. **How much does she put in each of these two categories?**

(Turn to page 29 for the answers)

CHAPTER FOUR

DO THE MATH: HELP! I'M OVER MY BUDGET

Your budget may look good on paper, but you will probably need to make adjustments for unexpected events.

Have you ever heard somebody say that an idea "looked good on paper"?

This means that plans don't always work out quite the way you had hoped.

A budget is a plan for how you will spend your money. But once the money is actually in your pocket, you may need to make adjustments to your budget.

Why? Life is full of unexpected events. For example, you leave your backpack on the city bus. You go to the bus company's lost

Is babysitting one of the ways you earn money?

and found office, but it's not there. You are going to have to buy a new backpack. That is an unexpected expense. And what do you do if the child you babysit every Saturday evening gets so sick that her parents decide to

stay home with her? Your income for the week will be lower. You're going

to have to adjust your budget to take that into account.

Washing cars is a job that young people can do to earn extra cash.

Megan stuck to her budget the first week, but then it fell apart the second week. On Tuesday, a neighbor asked Megan to do yard work on Saturday. She would earn $20.00 for the job. On Friday, Megan bought a pair of shoes on sale for $19.99. She borrowed the money from her mom, promising to pay her back with her earnings from the yard work. But then it rained all day Saturday, so Megan lost her job. Megan has to trim her budget so that she can pay for the unexpected expense. Trimming a budget means reducing expenses.

Megan's Budget for March 15 to March 31 (2 weeks)

CATEGORY	BUDGETED AMOUNT	ACTUAL AMOUNT	DIFFERENCE
FIXED INCOME			
Allowance $20.00 per week x 2	$40.00		
VARIABLE INCOME			
Chores for neighbors			
TOTAL	$40.00		
FIXED EXPENSES			
School lunches	$24.00		
Donation to animal shelter	$2.00		
Short-term goal	$2.75		
Long-term goal	$2.75		
VARIABLE EXPENSES			
School supplies	$0.75		
Snacks	$0.75		
Entertainment	$7.00		
TOTAL			

Megan owes her mom $20.00. They agree that Megan will pay her mother back at a rate of $4.00 per week. **How long will it take Megan to pay the money back?**

Megan looks at her budget. If she cuts entertainment in half, she will gain $3.50. **How much more does Megan need?** Remember, her budget is for two weeks.

Megan decides to cut her deposits for short- and long-term goals by $2.00 each. She will eliminate snacks entirely. **Has Megan balanced her budget?**

(Turn to page 29 for the answers)

Do you want to earn more income by doing jobs for neighbors? Try advertising. Create a flyer listing the jobs you will do and the prices for each. Distribute the flyer to family and friends and post it around the neighborhood.

When someone calls you about a job, remember that first impressions are important. Be professional. Show up on time. Be polite. After the job is done, don't forget to clean up. And be sure to say thank-you when you leave. A happy customer will recommend you to a freind

Tutoring younger students is another way to increase your income.

Another way to balance a budget is to earn more income. Think about ways you can earn more money. What jobs do you do at home? Maybe you can also do some of those jobs for neighbors. Good jobs for young people include dog walking, car washing, babysitting, and yard work. Are you a good baker, artist, or gardener? Maybe you could make something to sell.

Do you have skills you could teach others? Maybe you could give other kids lessons in computers or how to play basketball. There are many good books and Web sites that will help you think of ways to earn extra income.

There will be times when you need to pass up buying something you want in order to stick to your budget.

Megan likes doing yard work for neighbors, but it's supposed to rain for the next week. Rather than finding a new job, Megan decides to follow her tighter budget until she pays her mom back. This means it will take longer for her to save enough money to buy that new computer game she wants.

Though making her budget work was hard, Megan learned some good lessons. She learned that she needed to rework her budget to include an emergency fund. She decides to divide up her savings money. She plans to put away $2.00 each for short-term and long-term goals and to put $1.50 in a savings account for emergency expenses. Megan also learned what could happen if you spend money before you earn it!

BUDGETING AS A WAY OF LIFE

*If you stick to your budget, you will be able to put
money aside for expenses that you don't expect.*

Making a budget and sticking to it will bring many benefits. By keeping

to a budget, you will always have money for the things you need. With a

budget, you will also have money set aside to pay for unexpected expenses.

A budget is like a road map. You can see where you want to go and the

roads that will take you there. Most maps show you how many miles you

have to travel to reach your goal. As you head down the road, it's easy to

*Is there something you want to buy? Your budget is
your plan for reaching your financial goals.*

get sidetracked. You'll sometimes head off toward a place that looks like fun, but taking that detour keeps you from reaching your goal.

The same is true of your budget. A budget is your plan to reach your goal. The more money you spend on things you don't need, the longer it will take you to reach your goal. When you get paid, always pay for your basic needs and put money into your savings before you do anything else. Then the money that remains is yours to spend as you like. Putting money into savings first will allow you to take an occasional side trip and still end up at your goal on time.

21st Century Content

Sticking to a budget takes practice and effort. Here are some suggestions:

Keep your budget book and all of your receipts together.

Keep a money notebook for tracking your income and expenses.

Keep separate envelopes for savings, short-term goals, and long-term goals. Paste a picture of the item you are saving for on each envelope. It will remind you of your goal.

Keep larger amounts of money in the bank, where they will earn interest.

Having money saved up for emergencies will help you keep smiling even when life doesn't go as you planned!

Once in a while, when you go on a car trip, you'll get a flat tire. Having

a spare tire in the trunk is the best way to get back on the road quickly.

Make sure you always have that extra tire in the trunk. If you use it, replace

it as soon as possible, so you are ready for the next emergency.

An emergency savings account is like a

spare tire in the trunk. Set aside an amount

every month to use if emergencies come up.

An unexpected expense can take a long time

to pay off. It will keep you from reaching your

goals. Replace the emergency money as soon as

you can after using it. You want to be ready if

another flat tire slows you down!

Right now, adults pay for your basic needs of

food, shelter, and clothing. But when you get older,

you will have to pay for all your own expenses

with your own income. That's what it means to

be financially responsible. By managing a small

Learning & Innovation Skills

The United States government has the largest budget in the world. In 2007, the U.S. government planned to spend $2,770,000,000,000. That's nearly three trillion dollars. Its income in 2007 is predicted to be $2,416,000,000. Does the U.S. government have a balanced budget? The answer is no. It is over budget by $354 billion!

budget now, you will learn the skills to handle bigger budgets in the future.

Countries, counties, and cities all use budgets. So do businesses, schools, teams, and families. Learning how to make a budget and stick to it are skills you will use your entire life.

Many jobs require skills in making budgets and managing money.

REAL WORLD MATH CHALLENGE ANSWERS

Chapter One

Page 6

Megan's weekly expenses total $20.50.

$12.00 + $2.00 + $4.00 + 2.50 = $20.50

Megan's budget is not balanced.

$20.00 is less than $20.50

Chapter Two

Page 10

Megan's income was $77.25.

$30.00 + $20.00 + $7.25 + $20.00 = $77.25

Megan's expenses totaled $74.33.

$15.00 + $6.00 + $7.00 + $2.00 + $12.00 + $1.65 + $13.25 + $12.00 + $5.43 = $74.33

Megan spent $25.65 on needs, which were her lunch cards and school supplies.

$12.00 + $12.00 + $1.65 = $25.65

Megan's wants were clothes, movie, snacks, donation, CD, and souvenir. She spent a total of $48.68 on wants.

$15.00 + $6.00 + $7.00 + $2.00 + $13.25 + $5.43 = $48.68

Megan had a balanced budget.

$77.25 is greater than $74.33

Chapter Three

Page 15

In Megan's first budget, her expenses total $40.00.

$24.00 + $2.00 + $1.00 + $1.00 + $0.75 + $1.25 + $10.00 = $40.00

After lowering her entertainment and snacks budget, Megan's expenses total $36.50.

$24.00 + $2.00 + $1.00 + $1.00 + $0.75 + $0.75 + $7.00 = $36.50

This enables Megan to save an additional $3.50.

$40.00 − $36.50 = $3.50

Megan puts aside an extra $1.75 for short-term goals and an extra $1.75 for long-term goals, for a total of $2.75 in each category.

$3.50 ÷ 2 = $1.75

$1.75 + $1.00 = $2.75

Chapter Four

Page 18

It will take Megan 5 weeks to pay back her mother.

$20.00 ÷ $4.00 = 5

Megan needs to pay her mother $8.00 over two weeks. If she pays her mother $3.50 from her entertainment budget, she still owes her mother $4.50.

$4.00 x 2 (weeks) = $8.00

$8.00 − $3.50 = $4.50

After cutting short-term savings, long-term savings, and snacks, Megan has trimmed $4.75 from her budget. Her budget is now balanced.

$2.00 + $2.00 + $0.75 = $4.75

GLOSSARY

charity (CHEHR-uh-tee) an organization to help the needy or a gift to such an organization

deposits (dih-PAH-zutz) amounts of money put in a bank

fixed (FIKST) an amount that does not change

interest (IN-tuh-rest) the amount earned on money kept in a bank

variable (VAHR-ee-uh-bull) subject to change

volunteer (vah-lun-TEER) to do work without being paid

FOR MORE INFORMATION

Books

Donovan, Sandy. *Budgeting*. Minneapolis: Lerner, 2005.

Holyoke, Nancy. *A Smart Girl's Guide to Money: How to Make It, Save It, and Spend It*. Middleton, WI: American Girl, 2006.

Mayr, Diane. *The Everything Kids' Money Book: From Saving to Spending to Investing—Learn All about Money!* Cincinnati: Adams Media, 2000.

Web Sites

Hands on Banking

www.handsonbanking.org/

For an interactive program that teaches banking and money management skills

Kids.gov: Money

www.kids.gov/k_money.htm

Links to many government sites with information on money and banking for kids

PBS: It's My Life

pbskids.org/itsmylife/money/managing/article7.html

Money management information and games

INDEX

ABOUT THE AUTHOR

Cecilia Minden, PhD, is a literacy consultant and the author of many books for children. She is the former director of the Language and Literacy Program at Harvard Graduate School of Education in Cambridge, Massachusetts. She would like to thank fifth-grade math teacher Beth Rottinghaus for her help with the Real World Math Challenges. Cecilia lives with her family in North Carolina.